Advance Praise

This Visible Speaking creates a gorgeous polyphony of photographs, lyric meditations, and the voices of photographers. Image and text mirror each other, enacting the ways that the world of nature outside us can evoke and mirror our inner human life—our visions, loves, our losses. Like Georgia O'Keefe, Winograd says of her photos and forays into the wild, "I found I could say things with color and shapes that I couldn't say any other way—things I had no words for." Emily Dickinson writes of how "A light exists in spring" that "almost speaks to you"; in Winograd's book, it finally does. This is a book to hold close, to travel with—and return to—for a very long time.

—Angie Estes, author of *Parole*

Kathy Winograd's This Visible Speaking is a gorgeous foray into the splendors of her Colorado landscape, particularly the wildlife near and around the South Platte River. The beauty of snowy egrets, young flickers, cormorants, red-tailed hawks and other animals and growth caught in Winograd's camera-eye become astonishments. An essayist and poet Winograd's photographs of visual speaking are enriched by her lyrical conversations with the likes of Man Ray, Edward Weston, Paul Strand, and writers from Dante to Baudelaire, Poe, and Barthes. Like those artists she converses with, it is the transformative power of the visual, particularly when in dialogue with the textual, that rivets her. Having been gifted a camera during the Covid pandemic Winograd finds herself on a quest "looking for some kind of prayer" in what she describes as "translations of light" – a magic, her camera and poetry have so luminously gifted us.

—Adrianne Kalfopoulou, author of *On The Gaze and Ruin*

Out of the ash of grief and loss that COVID left behind for so many of us, Kathryn Winograd has assembled an astonishing book of prose and photographs. "I was looking for anything like prayer," she writes in her preface, "anything like visible parlare to bring back even a moment of peace, just a small quiet joy" and she has done more than that. She has caught "light through the camera's eye" and in every photograph is some shard of natural beauty from this fragile and resilient world that held us through a pandemic and holds us still. Her patient, quiet eye brings us fox, heron, owl, kestrel, painted turtles, butterflies, shells, orchids, and so much more. Kathryn Winograd's This Visible Speaking is a book with essays that honor and love the natural world—its birds and creatures, its fruits and flowers—and her book pays homage to other photographers and writers who share this holy regard. If praise is a form of prayer and prayer is a form of love, then these words and photographs are a love letter, touched by sadness and deep concern for the planet, yes, but not without a scintillating thread of hope for "what blossoms, what speaks."

—Lisa Zimmerman, author of *Light at the Edge of Everything*

This Visible Speaking

Catching Light Through the Camera's Eye

This Visible Speaking

Catching Light Through The Camera's Eye

Kathryn Winograd

THE HUMBLE ESSAYIST PRESS

Copyright © 2024 by Kathryn Winograd
All rights reserved.
No portion of this book may be reproduced in any form without written permission from the publisher or author, except as permitted by U.S. copyright law.

First edition. Published by The Humble Essayist Press

Hybrid Nonfiction/Poetry/ Photography
ISBN: 978-1-7345177-7-4
Author Photo: Will Sardinsky
Book Cover and Photo by Kathryn Winograd
Graphic Designer: John Hall
Book Photos: Kathryn Winograd

The Humble Essayist Press
254 Butternut Creek Rd
Blairsville, GA 30512

Always to Leonard
To Kitty and John for the unexpected gift
To Mira

To all those I follow in the search for light

Blue flax east of cabin.

from things we have imagined long familiar, a sudden intuition dawns.
— Jacob Burckhardt, 1868, founding father of art history

Contents

This Visible Speaking: An Introduction By Robert Root	1
Preface	3
1. Unlocking the Camera	7
2. Shooting a Snowy Egret at Blackrock Lake	11
3. On Beauty and Finding a Dead Flicker	15
4. Owl Head at Beaver Creek	19
5. Photographing the Wild Geranium	23
6. Widow Skimmer at Ladybug Lake	27
7. Moth Orchid at the Botanical Gardens	31
8. After Reading W. Henry Fox Talbot's Account Of How "Natural Objects Can Be Made to Delineate Themselves Without the Aid of the Artist's Pencil"	35
9. Our Rock Blossom Blooms	39
10. 3 a.m. and Taking the Puppy for a Pee Beneath a New Moon	43
11. Finding a Paper Wasp Nest Hanging Below a Porch Beam	47
12. Scrawled Cowfish Found on a Childhood Beach	51
13. Two Owls Dip Down from a Ponderosa Pine	55

14.	Histogram of the Fox in My Backyard	59
15.	Drawing with Light	63
	On the anniversary of my mother's death	
16.	Late Summer Wasps	67
	(And Not Bees)	
17.	Sweeping Dead Moths from a Window Screen	71
18.	Western Painted Turtles Sunning	75
	On the Submerged Tree my friend Called Holy	
19.	Photographing a Cabbage White Butterfly	79
	at Castlewood Canyon	
20.	Catching Light	83

Study Guide	87
Acknowledgments	89
About the Author	91
Endnotes	93

This Visible Speaking: An Introduction

By Robert Root

Genre crossing is an ancient form of expression. The twelfth-century scholar Bernardus Silvestris identified the third of his genres of composition as the "prosimetrical," works that braid together prose and poetry (his first two genres). Fusing elements of one literary, text-based genre with another literary, text-based genre occurs in Petronius' *The Satyricon*, Boethius's *Consolation of Philosophy*, and Dante Alighieri's *La Vita Nuova*. Matsuo Basho's celebrated haibun *The Narrow Road to the Interior* (Oko-no-Hosomichi) couples prose and poetry as a travel journal. Poetic attention to visual arts occurs in Keats's "Ode to a Grecian Urn" and Auden's Breughel-based "Musee des Beaux Arts;" Terry Tempest Williams' lyrical *Leap* wanders through Bosch's "Garden of Earthly Delights" triptych. Contemporary digital media has made text and image more immediately interactive. That's what Kathryn Winograd accomplishes in *This Visible Speaking*.

Each of the twenty sections of the book follow an engaging pattern: a vivid image, then a brief pertinent quote by a relevant artist or writer, then a lyrical journal entry, followed by a second image and a contemplative passage about her reading. Images and texts prompt interaction among one another, harmonizing with equal pertinence as we read the visual and survey the language. The challenge of combining visuals with text may be one of deciding whether the images illustrate the words or the words explain the images, thus in each case one serving as a supplement to the other, or whether the images and words are equally integrated and interdependent, as they are in this book. Successive portions spiral back into the portion that preceded them and forward into the portion that follows them.

As we quietly read the progression of images and texts, it doesn't take us very long to hear the visible speaking.

Preface

It was a morning during the quarantine, a morning almost like this one when I saw the first doe at the far edge of this same meadow in silhouette against the crater that our neighbor, dead two years now, bulldozed twenty years ago into the earth for the dirt we spilled around our newly-built cabin. I guessed then at the doe having given birth and stowing her fawn someplace close by our cabin. She was so solitary that whole spring and summer, yet stayed so near to us, worrying herself through the trees at my accidental approaches, but never fully vanishing like the other deer did, my clumsy walking scattering the herd to the gullies. Only at the summer's end did I realize that she had, indeed, given birth to not just one fawn, but twins, as I had decades past, her two freckled fawns one morning unfolding out of the summer light and grasses. I have no picture of that doe. Only memory. These words.

In the 14th century, Dante called the purest kind of beauty *visibile parlare*, this "visible speaking," in the second part of his *Divine Comedy*, when he climbs with Virgil up the Mount of Purgatory and sees three engravings on the mountain so vivid it seems that what is engraved could speak. The beauty is so great that it can only come from God's handiwork:

Colui che mai non vide cosa nova
produsse esto visibile parlare,
novello a noi perché qui non si trova.

his was the speech made visible by One
within whose sight no thing is new — but we,
who lack its likeness here, find novelty.
(*Purg*. 10.94-96)

Each time I think about that visible speaking, *visibile parlare,* I think Dante was talking about the images we humans attempt to create with our tongues and hands out of what we see and think beautiful in this world. But the images are beyond our capabilities, beyond all our efforts, and, instead, there is only Dante's God speaking to and through us. At the start of Covid, my daughter and son-in-law gave me a camera and my husband Leonard bought me a telescopic lens to capture what I saw at these places I love: our cabin at 9600 feet along Phantom Canyon where once trains, filled with gold, smoked the skies black, and the South Platte river near our suburban home in Littleton rife with heron and snowy egrets. The world changed for me at the river when the facilitator of a community naturalist class, zoomed because of Covid, asked me to go down to a wild place—of course, alone— and write down what I saw, heard, felt, and wondered. So I took my new camera to the river's edge, along with my journal and pen, to catch in the shutter's quick opening what I barely knew how to focus: broken milk pods and a striped water snake and the dark cormorants that perched daily on the silver bent back of a tree long drowned—for me, the visible speaking.

In my study, I collect the postcards I make out of the images I have captured. Each one is a living frame of time that I can lean on my windowsill. When Julia Margaret Cameron, an 1800s mother and housewife who became a master photographer, received the gift of a camera from her children, she wrote in her unfinished work, *Annals of My Glass House*, that from the moment she touched it, the camera became "as a living thing."[1] She turned her coal house into a dark room. Knowing nothing of the black box she held between her hands, she effaced her first photo by accidentally rubbing her hand over the "filmy side of the glass." But by the time she was photographing royalty like the Crown Prince and Crown Princess of Germany and Prussia and "friends" like the poet Alfred Lord Tennyson, her photographs had become to her "almost like the embodiment of a prayer."

I am not Julia Margaret Cameron, but I am looking for some kind of prayer. At sixty-four, I realize that I am at the age when my mother discovered she would go blind. At sixty-four, I am at the age when my father discovered he would descend into Alzheimer's. The written image is nothing new to me. I have written poetry since I was a child, reciting my poems to my mother, stationed at her typewriter, the mementos of my small life collected, turned into word. Even as I am writing these words, I am in a room I am making out of memory and love: the three bird pictures cross-stitched by my dead mother, the flower garden quilt hand-stitched by my great great grandmother and the small canvas panel painted by my great grandfather of a buck in antler. Perhaps this visible speaking, when it speaks from the photograph or the word, is always what speaks to the soul and what is Cameron's prayer: our re-creation of the world transmuted not by what we just see, feel, remember, wonder, but by whatever we call god .

The first time I posted a picture to Facebook— I don't remember which one it was— I remember my fear to do so and the instant embrace of it by a small group of friends online, whom I am ever grateful to. I was afraid to take classes and then I took classes and then I found myself writing at night about the camera images I took during the day, surprising myself with not, exactly, the *ekphrastic*, the time-honored, vivid description of a work of art,[2] but the chance pairings of photo and image, a drifting through language and memory into what might come out of a moment suspended forever by light and the sensory of a camera. In my research on how to take photographs, I stumbled over old classic essays, collected by Beaumont Newhall in *Photograph: Essays & Images*[3] and by Alan Trachtenberg in *Classic Essays on Photography*[4] about the earliest experiments with photography when an image was captured through light on copper or pewter plate or infused paper. I was drawn immediately to the lyrical writings of pioneers like William Henry Fox Talbot, who first pointed light toward paper and mourned the fleeting shadows he hoped to fix forever.[5] Unexpectedly, I found that the poets and writers I had known my whole life through the reading of literature, writers like the amateur photographer Oliver Wendall Holmes[6] and the poets Charles Baudelaire[7] and Edgar Allen Poe,[8] had written about photography, writing first about the daguerreotype, the beginnings of photography as we now know it. They had been passionately drawn into this sudden transformation of art and its communion, or, in Baudelaire's view, its "noncommunion," with this controversial new artist— the photographer.

Since Covid, my cameras tell me that I have taken thousands and thousands of photographs, mostly of the birds that haunt the cabin feeders and the riverbanks of the South Platte. I have collected here only a few photographs, the ones that spoke to me and set me to write at my study desk about the images and memories that arise from within, from unknown places. A few photos have found their way into the world: a cover photo for a literary journal, photos to accompany an essay or poems published online, and a place in a gallery exhibit at a children's hospital. I realized in putting this book together that the voices of those caught in the magic and mystery of those first renderings of light on pewter or copper and the later voices, as photography found its place in the arts, have a place in this book, too, their words so often as beautiful as any poet's. I followed the model of the naturalist's journal: its images and sketches, the notes and facts and observations the naturalist will jot down in the field or remember at the desk and the kitchen table. For this reason, I have placed each image and its title on a page alone, followed by a quote from those writers, artists, and inventors who greeted with astonishment and fear the changes that the discovery of fixing an image wrought by light permanently on a copper plate or treated cloth could create for the world. I follow the image with the reverie evoked for me. (Poem? Prose? I don't know nor care.) A small section of prose tells some of the history, the joy and trepidation that photography brought to those who first knew the awe-filled fixity of what they called "nature's pencil"— light. Endnotes provide the names and details of the many photographers, inventors, writers, artists, and philosophers I mention.

I have also rendered some of my photographs into watercolors, done through technology that I find delightful, but would be looked at askance by some of those 1800s pioneers who balked at the thought of photography as art in its original state, or, even worse, photography made to look more "painterly" through techniques that copied the "romantic" excesses of paintings meant to come from the soul and not just the eye. As you will see, my daughters balk at my "painting" through technology, but I find the finished results for some images airy and beautiful.

During that first year of Covid and the awful loss and loneliness it brought to the world, I was looking for anything like prayer, anything like *visibile parlare* to bring back even a moment of peace, just a small quiet joy after my mother died alone, and Leonard and I traveled twelve hundred miles across a country shut down to stand with my brother and his spouse alongside my father's grave and bury our mother's ashes, alone, without the rest of the family and the friends who loved her. I think I found a bit of that prayer when I saw that mother doe at the edge of our meadow, so momentary in the light. And now this morning, I have spotted another doe through the cabin window. She sleeps in the same late winter grass that the other doe, years past, slept in—I see the same silhouette of head and smooth prow of nose.

Such quiet this morning: even the meadows around the cabin and the Sangres to the west and the Arkansas Valley that drifts like a clouded sea below me are engulfed by what I imagine to be again this doe's slow quickening. Though I have no camera ready with me again, nothing to fix the doe by light into the beautiful forever, here, too, is the visible speaking, what I think now has always spoken to me, whether through the camera's eye or my own. I make my breakfast in silence, in slowness, lifting the tea kettle off the stove before its whistled steam and then carefully taking down a tea bag from the kitchen cabinet and placing it, so softly, in my teacup.

Unlocking the Camera

Bull elk hidden in the grass past Jan's old picnic table.

Notice to the Reader
The plates of the present work
are impressed by the agency of Light alone.
—William Henry Fox Talbot, *The Pencil of Nature*, 1844

Our key is a slip of metal, tiny and breakable. To keep the wildlife camera buoyant and steady above the *desire paths* not our own, where elk amble and a bobcat, a little nocturnal ghost we've caught twice on camera, preys on rabbit, we snug the camera lock's black winding cord over the nubs of lost branches. A "tree's self-pruning," my daughter assures me—nothing to wax over like loss, nothing to grieve. This is the bliss, I once read: the body and the being within magnified by the lens of a camera we can hold in our hands or tie to a tree. No, we once said, there's nothing more to see, nothing wild beyond us, but look! in the camera's eye—the tip of an antler, the bowed neck of a deer, the yellow haunch of a lion my neighbor once said he hunted down thirty of. And now a flicker swoons past and a woodpecker hooks itself to a tree, and, there!—the little bear the dogs once treed and I clapped at through the dark woods until my hands stung. And, oh, the last long snow, not cold to our touch at all now, but gilding everything, wind brush by wind brush.

Eighty-three years after the first public newspaper account appeared of Louis Daguerre, who invented the daguerreotype, the first photograph image made from silver-sheeted plates of copper and vaporized iodine, and his technique for "[fixing] the images which paint themselves within a camera obscura,"[1] Edward Weston observed: "The finest nuances of light and shade may be captured in the magic silver, and at the very instant desired—not when memory has to rebuild—perhaps crudely—the past."[2] Yet I keep finding how that very instant sparks memory and, perhaps, even changes memory. Roland Barthes, a French essayist and literary theorist, said that the photograph at its simplest is simply the past—what was— and that "this is its pathos, its melancholy": it is "without future."[3] William Henry Fox Talbot, considered by some to be the British inventor of photography, argued in "The Open Door" perhaps for the same sense of reality in the "daily and the familiar"—the painter's eye or the photographer's stopped by what others saw as ordinary.[4] Ironically, only twenty-five of Daguerre's own daguerreotypes exist. All I know is this: when I walk the world with a camera in hand now, I find everything stops me, every agency of light, every visible speaking.

Deer Selfie in the wildlife camera east of the cabin in the gully, watercolor.

Shooting a Snowy Egret at Blackrock Lake

Snowy Egret I startled flying over Blackrock Lake.

People will form collections of all kinds, which will be the more precious because art cannot imitate their accuracy and perfection of detail; besides, they are unalterable by light.
—Louis Jacques Mande Daguerre, *"Daguerreotype," 1839.*

What the camera wants is something maybe beautiful, maybe high-stepping the moon's low tide, something to focus, to slow-shutter into a stillness my palm can hold. Or maybe it just wants the silver fishhooks and the lost spinners or the feathered jigs I've watched the morning fishermen snag then snip free. All wild and danger-fraught I thought this river: this picking through the pipes and stems of old bird bones or the broken flasks of gin and berry wine I drank wild one college night, riding in a grocery cart because of some lost love that means nothing to me now. Here, at the river, this gravel pit turned to a lake is a vacancy stowed at the elbow of a huge highway I cannot unhear. An egret of snow stabs yellow foot after yellow foot into the littered water, then stalls. This camera, far beyond my sad eye, clicks and clicks. Crawdads and, maybe, sunfish, and even the bluegills floating above the pearl eggs in my father's pond are here at my touch—something to come of exposure, something to come of light.

Snowy egrets preening in the South Platte River.

The first ekphrastic connection between word and object through vivid description of the seen was by the poet Horace in his poem, "Ars Poetica"—utpictura poesis— "as is painting so is poetry." One translation, I think: poetry, as "imaginative texts," deserves the same critical attention as painting. When Dante in his Cantos on Purgatory spoke of "esto visibile parlare," this visible speaking, he was speaking of the grandeur of God in all things, even human-made: through everything beautiful is God speaking to us. I knew none of this. I had only seen the snowy egrets at Blackrock Lake for the last few years and so I simply photographed them, not knowing what might begin. And then, a summer later, tubing exploded in the South Platte River, banishing the snowy egrets from these favorite rocks. Now, I have the memory of these egrets turned to image to word— moments of ekphrasis, translations of light.

On Beauty and Finding a Dead Flicker

Young flicker I found on the cottonwoods at the South Platte River.

But the artist, even in photography, must go beyond discovery and the knowledge of facts.
He must create and invent truths...
— Albert Sands Southworth, "The Early History of Photography in the United States," *1871.*[1]

I've been thinking about beauty and how these bluebirds keep throwing themselves off the aspen snags ahead of me. Like a hinge, the wanting mind already calling them 'beautiful" and "sky," though I don't know really what beauty is or how to make it so in a poem about a gravel lane I keep writing about. Leonard never sees the bluebirds, though he wants to, but every day these past few days I have walked into them, little sky chips I might touch. I remember Leonard telling me how, when he was a boy, his mother taught him to sing for her friends: a song about pockets and catching stars. When he sings it to me now, we are happiest. In just this hour, fall has towed in its clouds like blue barges. Beautiful. And I am remembering the earliest summer morning, not here, not now, but as far away as childhood: tree swallows flushing above the sedge and a guttering of flickers. And now at my feet, there is this perfect silhouette of a flicker in the dirt I thought to photograph because there was light and there were wings and nothing to grieve, neither door nor earth.

Remnants of the flicker I found along the two-wheel lane to Mike's cabin, watercolor.

In 1859, Charles Baudelaire lamented the then-current painter's inclination to paint what he sees in the style of the photographer and not the dreamer. The society in the dawn of photography, Baudelaire said, "rushed, like Narcissus, to contemplate its trivial image on the metallic plate [of the photograph]."[2] Fearing the awe photographs created with their faithfulness to reality and truth, Baudelaire argued that photographs served best to "save crumbling ruins from oblivion, books, engravings, and manuscripts, the prey of time." He shuddered at the thought of the photograph being allowed to intrude on what he called the "intangible and the imaginary" and doubted the photographer's ability to "add something to it from his soul," which the painter could. What do I find in the language of doors and earth now provoked by an image I saw and took, if not with something, with some dream, some dream of the self?

Owl Head at Beaver Creek

Owl's head I found at Beaver Creek on the rocking chair I painted for the cabin porch.

If such a picture is rubbed or even lightly touched, or subjected to the pressure of a roller, it is destroyed past redemption; but, who could imagine anyone pulling apart a fine piece of lace or brushing the wings of a butterfly?
   —Dominique François Arago *from his 1839 report on the proposal to grant a lifetime pension to M. Daguerre (and his son) for his invention.*[1]

I watched a red-tailed hawk—what I wanted to write about here first— plummet from a telephone wire above a suburban bicycle path: a conical of wings, a silken hood of air bronzed in the light. And tender-necked, too, the hawk astride its prey so quickly, a whole raft of wings in the grass tips afloat. I found the owl later, below Skaguay Reservoir where it drains into Beaver Creek and where cow hooves pock the sludge of the riparian. A feathered thing in the grass I toed until I turned it over, thinking it a gosling dead. Its eyes were heavy-lidded, dreaming as if the owl were still drowsy from the fall, its body gone, only the head for me to cradle home, calling out to Leonard, *here, here*. Don't ask me why I think this: but how wild, my love, we once were, how blossomed we must have seemed to the wheeling hawks, to those smooth blades of the sky we still lift our faces to, white and dark our flesh.

Red-tailed hawk flying through cottonwood grove along the suburban drainage ditch.

One hundred years after the first daguerreotypes were presented to the French Académie des Sciences in 1839, Paul Valéry, a poet, presented "The Centenary of Photography" to the French Academy, calling photography a tool to help the writer remember what he saw.[2] A little less than a hundred years later, I walked along Beaver Creek, below the spillway of Skaguay Reservoir. Summer, I think it was, the riparian flooded where the cattle had walked. Further down the path, I found that explosion of feathers. Hawk or coyote, I said, killed it, though Leonard said most likely another owl. I brought the owl head back to the cabin and left it in the woodpile to dry. Weeks later it disappeared and I have only this image I took with my phone left, a moment caught in what Valéry called, "quick takes." As Valéry says, "All the rest is literature," that what I imagine are "mere constructions . . . bodiless . . . invisible to the photographic eye "—what I have written, what I will remember alongside these photographs.

Photographing the Wild Geranium

Wild Geranium by the spring in the gully west of the cabin.

Wherever there is light, one can photograph.
— Alfred Stieglitz, 1864-1946.[1]

I thought to take a picture of something flown, of something like the goldfinch I saw riding a sunflower by a quick river I passed the other day. But a teaspoon of light drew me to my knees, the sun pulling me into this weedy gulch to lie beneath petal veins and five lavender lobes. The camera dials and buttons I turn and click trespass too loudly in this late afternoon near a little spring for a cow or an elk or something else, its waters muddied still, I think, by what drank or bathed just before me. It's said of Stieglitz that "the humblest object appears to be, for him, instinct with marvellous life."[2] I laid my whole self down beneath a wild geranium where rain still lingers. Someone named the geranium *cranesbill*, what I kneeled at, half-wild and yoked there seed by seed. When will the river come again? And the white egret I saw quiet at its edge?

By chance, I once wrote in a journal— how many years ago I don't know— that for fifteen years coyotes ran the cabin gully "beneath my midnight window, singing/ wild/ chaotic/ darkness and moon beauty speaking." And by chance, I came across Alfred Stieglitz, not just the father of modern photography, but the husband and photographer of Georgia O'Keeffe, whom he photographed hundreds of times in the name of the Modernist's fragmented self, that flux of personality and world that one interrupts only fleetingly through image.[3] Photographer's or poet's image, I think— essence and meaning found in not just the thing itself, but the artist, too, despite the fears of so many in the early 1800s with that first spill of sunlight on nitrate of silver. I took the picture of this lone poppy by the cabin porch with a macro lens, this blossom seeded there by me, by chance, I don't know how long ago: an eruption of stamen—reminder, for me, of those feminine and sexual images I love in O'Keeffe's work: Orchid and Light Iris, Abstract Blue, *and* Two Calla Lillies on Pink. *"You are so much to me that you must not come to me," Stieglitz once wrote to O'Keeffe, in his wooing of her. "Coming may bring you darkness instead of light—And it's in Everlasting light you should live."[4] Darkness and moon beauty speaking, I think.*

Pink poppy I planted by the cabin porch.

Widow Skimmer at Ladybug Lake

Widow Skimmer poised near Ladybug Lake by the South Platte River.

*The gift from those I loved so tenderly added more and more impulse
to my deeply seated love of the beautiful, and from the first moment I handled my lens
with a tender ardour.*
—Julia Margaret Cameron, "Annals of My Glass House," *1874.*

I heard Leonard whistling this morning in the basement when I was checking my camera lens, his symphony climbing note by note up from the basement stairs. I don't know what music fills him exactly as he pedals to infinity on his stationary bike each day. But the sound of his whistling always drives me back mid-country, through fields of maize and soybean when I was younger than our daughters are now and I hardly knew him, the two of us driving toward love, I suppose, in a car he had to tie shut with a clothesline, Leonard whistling us into a first kiss and now our forty years vanishing as quick as our storm door shuts behind me. Now light swells through the river air and the clouds of milk pod I click my camera at. Who am I, I wonder, in my husband's whistling crescendos and then in this silence without him? Such ruin, if I let myself think it: the wetness of a coming autumn or even the white fire of an egret. I want to keep hearing him, his whistle trilling Chopin or Beethoven long before the radio fires up, the air he conducts eyes closed all cymbal-clash and snare drum, tender violin. A dragonfly rises over this river and the lost fishing hooks I keep stumbling over. Light, oh, light, even a finger's length: this widow skimmer once wheeling in tandem with another beneath the plunging kingfisher —love, sudden love— *light of god*, I've heard it called, dipping through the seed heads.

Cormorants at winter sunset on Eaglewatch Lake.

These dark color bands on the wings of the male widow skimmer I keep looking at are called "mourning crepe." As my daughter and son-in-law gave me my camera, so the daughter of Julia Margaret Cameron gave her mother a camera with the words: "It may amuse you, Mother, to try to photograph your solitude at Freshwater." As I am amused. "I long to arrest all the beauty that came before me," Julia Margaret Cameron said and so her journey into photography began. She is considered a master portraitist, though critics, at the time, complained about her lack of technique. The woman, who said she began not even knowing "where to place my dark box," later shot portraits of the poet Alfred, Lord Tennyson and Charles Darwin. This afternoon at the river, I noticed how the wind had changed sound: it is no longer a sea within the pine trees, but something louder, multitudinous, many-voiced.

Moth Orchid at the Botanical Gardens

Moth Orchid I photographed at the Botanical Garden's greenhouse.

The grammar and language of art can be taught, but it is quite different with its poetry.
—Henry Peach Robinson, "Idealism, Realism, Expressionism," 1896.[1]

I don't know why this morning this matters, awake so much of the night worrying over what loves me, what not. I only opened a tiny slice of the camera's aperture, so caught by the orchid's pink lip, its quill curl, its petals half-swerved as if a moth, white as the common cabbage butterfly I've known, eased through the air. "Gorgeous," my friend wrote, the orchid digital I sent him, called *Moth,* a crater in the pixels, an illumination in the hot house background of the botanical gardens I muted and blackened until I could orchestrate the photograph into something other than just *moth*. Maybe *moon* or, better yet, the teeth from the remains of the six-year-old the anthropologists call *Naledi,* little star.[2] The enamel's like ours, but the child is not quite human in some eyes, her child pearls fixed deep into the earth on a cavern ledge, arrayed there 240,000 years ago by what we don't know. Now this century, a small woman's hand has plucked Naledi's teeth from the earth, from this cave called *Rising Star*. Maybe it was some earth fracture the child catapulted through—or, maybe better, mourned she was ferried down the stone maze in love. This orchid barely kindles by seed, but even it is not omnipotent. Too dark for this, I think, to tell the myth of a boy dismantled rib by rib into an orchid flower that feeds upon the air. I remember how I dialed the camera's exposure back as if I would take the picture wrong, adjusted shadow and contrast until a satellite bud leaked out beside its moth moon. There is a moth I've heard of that gathers to the cavernous dark and not to light, tissue its wings that plummet into dreams and half-histories. Oh, this story is too complex now: a cabbage moth riding out the dark that I composed and a flower moon a hundred million years old dusting me with feather seeds I cannot see. The moth orchid breaks into pieces and birds fly them to root in lonely places. Or they plunge into everything I think beautiful.

House Finch feeding in the backyard redbud tree, watercolor.

In the 20th century, Man Ray, a painter of surrealism and dadaism, rediscovered the cameraless photograph, distilling his images by placing an object on photographic paper and directing to it light.[3] He called his creations "rayographs." Man Ray entered the ongoing debate between painting and photography as art by saying that he only painted what came from "imagination or from dreams" and photographed what already existed. I wonder what doesn't already have an existence that I've seen? I keep thinking of what Walter Benjamin, philosopher and critic who killed himself to escape the Nazis, said about the "optical unconscious," that how different what "speaks to the camera than speaks to the eye."[4] In the image, the past and the future burn through, "a spot... held together unconsciously." The photographer's unconscious and the poet's, where, as in Man Ray's rayographs, dreams exist, burn light and shadow, I think, on whatever the heart can bear.

After Reading W. Henry Fox Talbot's Account

Of How "Natural Objects Can Be Made to Delineate Themselves Without the Aid of the Artist's Pencil"

Black-crowned night heron in snow I surprised at Eaglewatch Lake near the South Platte River.

When I saw how beautiful were the images which were thus produced by the action of light, I regretted the more that they were destined to have such a brief existence.
—William Henry Fox Talbot, *"Some Account of the Art of Photogenic Drawing," 1839.*

I go at dinner time, summer evening before nightshade and the persistent red-eyed sun poised just above the foothills— a stoplight in the smoke and ozone of this wildfire year. I pull into the gravel parking lot on the south side of the reservoir, the "wild" side where speed boats and water bikes don't dare venture past the warning signs for low water and hidden objects. This time the riparian cusp between river and woodland, between marsh and the field where the rangers lead out plodding strings of summer horses, has shrunk so much that the ridge at the knife edge of trees rises above the water like a fin. What means the most to me here? I remember watching, just a few days earlier, a young boy paddling his kayak after his father, who was far ahead of him, and he yelled into the very trees where I, too, have paddled after everything. I think of Talbot lamenting over his first "photogenic drawings," and, so, it is in this silence that I watch the long-boned herons in the rookeries of egret.

Night Heron hunting in the shore bushes at Eagle-watch Lake, watercolor.

Talbot first used nitrate of silver to create an image on paper. Sunlight on the paper would turn the nitrate of silver dark while the shadow of an image would remain white. He, at first, could only view his images by candlelight—daylight destroyed every image he created. Then he finally hit upon the combination of a salt solution on the paper that sometimes transformed the "shadow-image," as he called it, into shades of lilac. He discovered, too, that a wash of iodine turned the image to "very pale primrose yellow," which, when set near the heat of a fire, turned a "full gandy yellow." Cold, the image returned to light. Perhaps I am drawn to the sometimes transformation of the photographic image into watercolor, which my daughters protest because it represents the blurred vision of imagination, and the image I leave there on the page is like a hinge between reality and dream-making.

Our Rock Blossom Blooms

Old lichen growing on a granite boulder near our spring south of cabin.

*To myself, the greatest charm of photography is the happy way
in which it will render the feeling of light, the sense of space,
and of atmosphere, the beauties of opposing lights and darks.*
—Frederick H. Evans, "On Pure Photography," *1900.*[1]

I don't know why I thought of her this morning, up here in our cabin without you, the snow you guessed yesterday to fall floating swollen and drowsy past this kitchen window. So early I woke to walk outside and fill the bird feeders. At our little meadow's edge, a doe lay quiet in the yellow grass. It was then I thought of the rocks and how we said they bloomed and of our suburban neighbor, how she unleashed every spring with her bulbs and flowerings—our own green-thumbed Demeter striding across our mown lawns, the lilies' paper bulbs swinging at her hip. She would dangle them in gift above my head where I knelt in such a fever of weeds and a pyre of dandelion, my young body still hungry for some other birth. What can I tell our daughters about love? Our love? (Decades since I cried above an earth I thought cold.) Maybe how it buries and unburies itself, secreted only until something tenders it out: a doe rooted in spring snow, a rag of pretty moss.

Stellar Jay waiting for a spot at the cabin feeder, watercolor.

I find this statement by the early 1900s photographer Paul Strand: "At every turn, the attempt is made to turn the camera into brush."[2] My daughters complain that the images in my photographs that I turn to watercolor, through technology, not the artist's hand, are "not real." And yet I've come to love the transformation of image from photo to the written word to watercolor: the world I discover in a granite rock or a raindrop or preening of a bird made beautiful anew, again and again, and again. Photographers like Paul Strand, who broke from the Photo-Secession's manipulation of the photographic negative into vestiges of fine art paintings, called for the simplicity of the technology, the absolute of the camera eye. Edward Weston said, "The finished print must be created in full before the film is exposed." I, the photographer, must learn to see "photographically," only then can I reveal "essence."[3] Yet I choose in these watercolors what evokes something in me, even the "pretend" artist's hand transforming something into other. Perhaps it is just as the poet William Carlos Williams said: "Now the grass, tomorrow/the stiff curl of wildcarrot leaf/One by one objects are defined."[4]

3 A.M. and Taking the Puppy for a Pee Beneath a New Moon

Moon Shell I found on a Cape Cod beach.

*Photography enables [us] to reveal the essence of life before [our lens]
with such clear insight that the beholder may find the recreated image
more real and comprehensible than the object.*
—Berenice Abbott, "Photography at the Crossroads," 1951.[1]

It was the 3:00 a.m. mewling, the new puppy nudging me into the suburban dark and moon milk, that made me think of the moon snail propped on my study window sill between the photos of the moth orchid and Wilson's snipe I fashioned into postcards. How long has this moon snail gathered dust there, shifted my afternoon sun to richest shadow? Nameless to me once at the edge of tidal spume and broken cockle shells but now a spiral perfect of nipple-brown apex and hollow umbilicus. Leonard keeps asking me why we are here. Why this cup of tea? he asks. Why this pen beneath a soda straw width of galaxies uncountable? Nights, the predatory moon snail plows nocturnal shores and drills the shells of clams with holes we string and wear. It lays a thousand eggs into collars of sand, shaped, we say, into ones our priests wear. For this puppy, unlike us— everything is new: the curly cues of dried snail and earthworm beneath the gutter spout, the blue bachelor button in bloom it chews happily at the driveway's edge. Once conjured by my camera into dark and shadow, this moon snail pixelated into swirls of pigeon-blue and rose-flesh: somewhere, someplace else, there is a constant sea rain of tiny moon snails and this moon, too, here, where beneath it my puppy and me, just us, blink.

My "Dead Box" I found in my father's Indiana hayloft and filled with my scatterings.

I discovered that one of the first daguerreotypes was Louis Daguerre's "Shells and Fossils" in 1839. One of the first news accounts of the daguerreotype marveled at how "M. Daguerre has found the way to fix the images, which paint themselves within a camera obscura, so that these images are no longer transient reflections of objects."[2] This image was black and white: three wooden shelves filled with shells and fossils. Everything I loved was photographed, there, on three shelves. My own shells I found washed up on the beach, some still with the living snail in them. Flies swarmed the moon snail I found and I knew it dead and loved it still for its spiraling nipple and ancient sea scars. Georgia O'Keeffe painted "Red Hills and White Snail"—not my moon shell, as I thought, but the nautilus. The critics say the organic objects she painted, including the shells she had collected since girlhood, as I collected mine, perhaps in their abstraction, symbolize her "emotions." Of her own work O'Keeffe said, "I found I could say things with color and shapes that I couldn't say any other way—things I had no words for."[3]

Finding a Paper Wasp Nest Hanging Below a Porch Beam

Paper wasp nest from my suburban porch now on top of my Dead Box.

The camera will become smaller and smaller,
more and more prepared to grasp fleeting secret images...
—Walter Benjamin, "Short History of Photography," *1931.*

This morning, before your arrival at our cabin, I found myself touching early lupine—wild, poisonous to dog and child— and, then, the scarlet paintbrush, *prairie fire,* beneath the fence barbs. It's almost too beautiful—that word again—to write: the summer all leaf light and wounded grass in the gully where rain has bowed down the seed heads. And now this tailing I found of last spring when each new queen awakened in its glass comb. How many years have I almost touched paper wasp nests I've found to the palms of children when I teach them the names of poetry and fragile worlds: *mud dauber* and *mole's hand*, *chrysalis* and *owl pellet*? Last night, locking the doors for bed, so utterly alone it felt, I startled the crescent moon at the north window pane. It made me think of my mother, so long widowed, how she pushed the cuticles of her nails down with a piece of metal, swift jabs, then scoured the tops of her nails short and flat. Tonight you peel your nightly apple, what I'll remember too, seed-star at the center I split into decades ago for our daughters, such old love we have riding the light, the counted days. Sometimes by just wing brush the paper wasps pollinate what blossoms, what speaks.

Skeletal mole's hand I found as a child at my father's Indiana farm.

As late as the 1970s, (and still happening probably now, but I haven't yet discovered it in my searchings), discussion over the nature of photography versus the nature of fine art and its paintings by the human hand has continued. John Berger, a writer and critic, who explored our "ways of seeing," argues in his essay, "Understanding a Photograph," that at its most basic, the photograph simply represents what the photographer thought worthy of capturing.[1] What is as important as what has been photographed, then, is what has not been photographed. Photography, which does not transform what it gives us, contains all and, hence, becomes part of an "ideological struggle," a vision of total reality that the photographer has chosen to give us. What does it mean then that I have placed a paper wasp nest and then an old hand of a mole on an old jewelry box I call the Dead Box to take their pictures? What does it say about what we live amidst and what we lose and never see? I've kept the mole's hand for fifty years now because I thought it minuscule, nailed, and human.

Scrawled Cowfish Found on a Childhood Beach

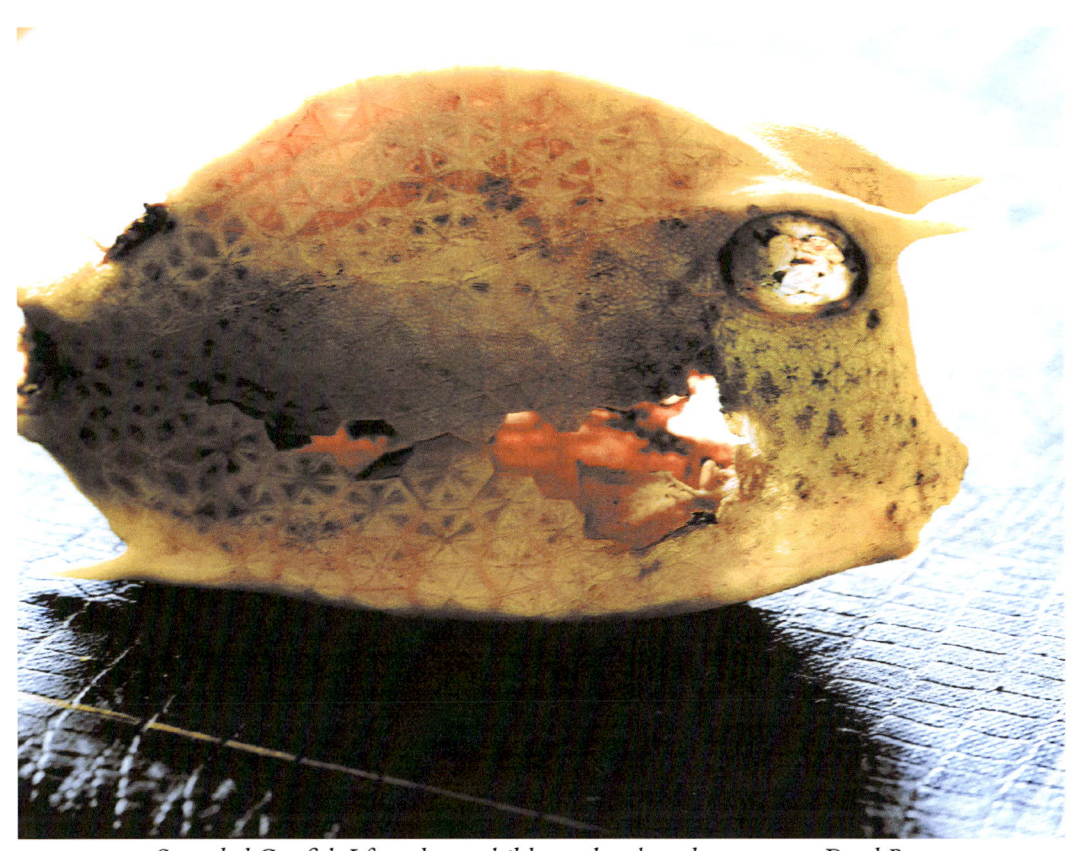

Scrawled Cowfish I found as a child on a beach and now on my Dead Box.

Photography is, after all, too profoundly interwoven with the deep things of Nature to be entirely unlocked by any given method.
—Lady Elizabeth Eastlake, "Photography," *1857*.[1]

Sometimes I am reminded so clearly of how I live in a strange and beautiful world where unexpected moons buoy out of the eastern horizon, where jet contrails my ancestors never saw strewed the sky like artist strokes. And stones circle the earth. Once, sitting in my daughter's Chicago apartment, not knowing if it were morning or night, I wondered how many others see the moon rise out of a pine tree or a smear of clouds until the moon's light spills to the ground and it is as if day, our night shadows there. Edward Weston said that "only the photographer can register what lies between himself and the object before his lens." Somewhere then, someone else is stepping down a silver ladder—I've done it once— the side of a boat slick with salt, a knife heat of silver on the seawater, and the body going under foot arch then knee hollow, hip crease and trembling belly, now the old buds of the breasts floating. I remember now how I broke free and pushed the suck of the snorkel mask down into light and green and sapphire blue— the clear strobes of jellyfish, beautiful, and empty.

If I can't etch it beautiful, the pen slipping useless as floe ice along the page, I'll snap the image to a pixel and the shining back of a card. The French inventor Nicéphore Niépce in 1826 used the camera obscura to project from his bedroom window the first known photographic image onto a pewter plate coated with bitumen of Judea. Ever since then, with his blurred light of "Point de Vue du Gras," there seems to have been an insistence in the critical history of photography on identifying what can be called beauty or art or none. William M. Ivins, Jr. argues that only the photograph is able to show the true surface of an object of art: "their bosses, hollows, ridges, trenches, and rugosities."² It was these telltale details that caught the movement of the artist's hand. All I know is that, sometimes, I can't remember anyone's words, not even mine, the night pulsing outside my window with a legion of crickets, tawny throats to send me sleep. Knees bent, I have edged close to the bedrock of a train track, camera in hand, where trains once traveled filled with silver or gold bound to the crumbs of this granite I have scraped my knees through. Just what have I disposed from air? The spotty veins of an orchid? A water snipe, the long twig of its beak? Or a moon snail wound up from the nipple tip of its umbilicus, every hue, blue dark and sand craven, dipped, I still think, as if in azure, and shining?

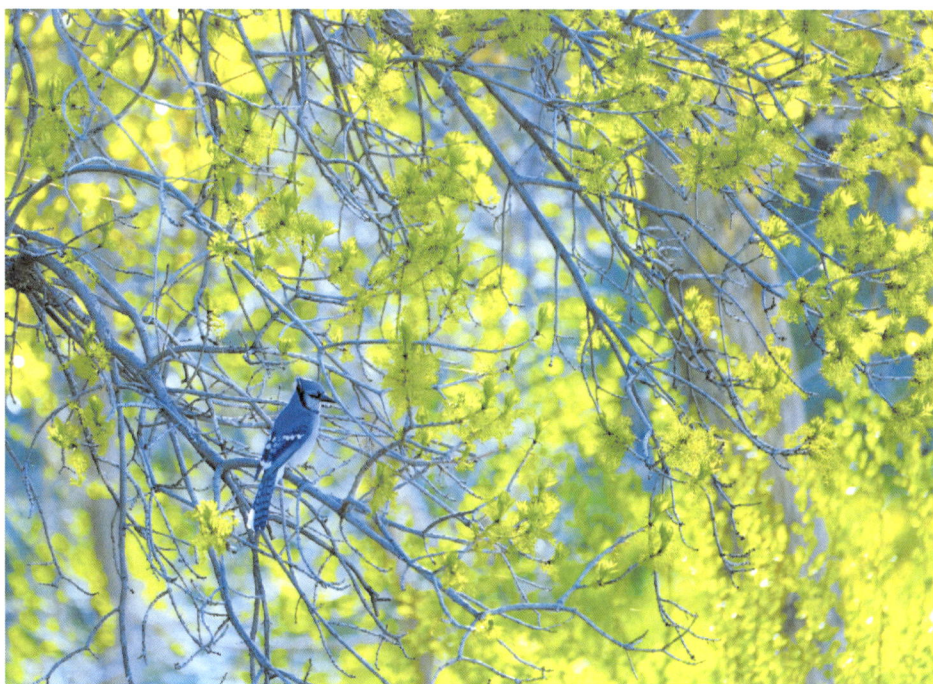

Blue Jay resting in the cottonwood trees near our suburban drainage ditch.

Two Owls Dip Down from a Ponderosa Pine

Great Horned Owl mother in suburban cottonwood grove near bike trail.

This is the most delicate of all the processes. Experience alone can teach the time required with different objects in a different light.
—*Oliver Wendell Holmes,* "*Doings of the Sunbeam,*" *1863.*

The owl dipped down from the ponderosa pine, level-winged and soft arc, to the miner's candle and the woods' rose I keep touching. And then it glided up toward tall trees and gold-glittered granite someplace far from me. A second owl followed, just to the left of me, its white feathers, just visible, a softness, a floating. Why had I not been looking up? Once I lived with everyone else in a pandemic. People died; people didn't. Now the hummingbirds trill past the feeders and evening grosbeaks gather yellow-masked, in tandem, their goldenrod breasts like shatterings. I watch the birds. I step quietly through the woods, half-fearful of the silence. A grasshopper sparrow darts from its grass nest, three brown speckled eggs at my feet, all life and waiting, and in the small grove, where I have walked so blindly, twin fawns, shadow and light, unfold. I remember the yellow warblers that once quickened in some berried bushes. And how someone said to me, "I thought it was a pear," when I caught one, momentary, in the light.

An owl in our suburban tree was the last to sit there. Strangled, weeping dead pine needles, our Ponderosa succumbed to beetle or tip moth and we cut it down. It was David Octavius Hill's portrait photos in 1843 that Walter Benjamin spoke of—the "Newhaven Fishwife"—the fishwife who would later slash her wrists after the birth of her sixth child: "The spark has, as it were, burned through the person in the image with reality, finding the indiscernible place in the condition of that long past minute where the future is nesting."[1] I caught this yellow warbler in the aspen chute in the gully east of the cabin, an image someone called a pear. Someone unknown said, "…the artist really never composes at all; he merely hunts nature for bits to make into such a whole as he has once actually seen, but which he was unable, owing to its fleetness…".[2] As artist, as poet.

Yellow Warbler flocking at the aspen shoot east of the cabin.

Histogram of the Fox in My Backyard

Fox sunning apart from her den and kits in my suburban garden.

There is no instant of time not fully bound and related to every other.
—Paul Rosenfeld, *"Stieglitz," 1921.*

The fox leapt over the backyard fence onto the roof of our empty dog house, all golden in the morning and in the haze of the window screen I steadied my camera at. A gift, Leonard said, a visitor like the poet D.H. Lawrence's snake: "out the dark door of the secret earth." It bedded down on the roots of a perennial I mulched last year, so much the gift itself— this gold webbing through the screens. A poet I told warned me that the fox was a killer, a "skulk of foxes," he said he had titled his own fox poem. How it hurts to love the earth sometimes, the things of it. We kept exclaiming at the window as the fox curled around itself, snoozed in the sunlight. *Grace,* I might have called it, though who knows its fealty to the bruised heart. I could barely see the fox, my eyes still too dried from a night's sad toll, but it lives now in this picture I made out of pixels—not of film or chemicals or silver wash or mercury, like those tiny beads of silver that slipped from a thermometer I broke long ago, my mother hushing me aside, every gradient shining here. The eyes of the fox are almost amber as if they were river water churning with fish eggs or the broken down leaves you can see, breathless, from the shallows up. The fox stayed another night, a quick little fire. We feared it might be sick, but in the morning, fat and saucy, it tossed pine cones around the backyard. I think I told that poet I was in the grip of gods and gifts, not the murderous, something instead like St Francis of Assisi lugging not a staff but my 400 mm lens.[1] Click and click: the fox all gold in the morning light and then a magpie on the fence top flicking its head at the fox, chiding it for spilling all that gold glory.

Fox mother standing in the suburban garden, watercolor.

Andre Bazin, the French film critic, begins his essay, "The Ontology of the Photographic Image," with the Egyptians who artificially preserved man in death as a way to "snatch it from the flow of time."[2] Now, Bazin says, image-making is about creating the ideal with its own construct of time—a "temporal destiny" that is unique from reality. A fox walked into our suburban backyard, a stay of rest from its den-buried kittens and I took the camera and shot it through the window screen, past dust mote, moth wing, and slender spider leg while my visiting great niece and nephew squealed and clapped. All of us— fox, children, me, the detritus of a moment, a destiny— still here.

Drawing with Light

On the anniversary of my mother's death

Red-tailed Hawk I caught lifting off from our suburban cotton grove.

Some people are still unaware that reality contains unparalleled beauties.
—Bernice Abbott, "Photography at the Crossroads," 1951.

Everything is light now, driving down Phantom Canyon into a storm's blessing, rivulets like water lilies cut across the whole road of it. And there, by our shed, where painted ladies—*Vanessa cardui*—sometimes hundreds float, the spotted knapweed I weed-whacked down the week before nod again beneath the rain's weight, our meadow purple-flooded, and beneath the pines *butter-and-eggs* blossoming. The morning aspens give me shadows and red-capped russula, milky caps. I thought the birds, the smallest ones, had caught the air thermals toward the valleys and the great scissor curves of rivers they shadow, only the raptors left—coopers and red-tailed hawks, the bald-faced turkey vulture. But yellow birds scatter in the woods, ride the fall's dieback. Late afternoon, almost golden hour, a bull elk grazes up the hill past Jan's old picnic table and I follow it quietly as I can, *gone*, I keep thinking, and then the antlers staggered as blue penstemon, rise above the grass. I had forgotten the names of field grass my mother knew— *wildrye* and *June grass*, *fox barley* and *sedge*— but now I know them: this day lush, end of summer, wind and din of wasp wild. Leonard said he dreamed the dead back and they were smoothed by joy.

Great Blue Heron scratching itself at Eaglewatch Lake, watercolor.

The root words for photography come from the Greek words, photo *and* graph, *meaning "light" and "to draw." Why the expression "drawing with light"? Or writing with light? Today, I discovered that there is a whole series of photographs by Picasso known as his "Light Drawings."*[1] *He held a small light in his hand and drew it through the air, his drawings of light caught by the photographer Gjon Mills, who kept the shutters of two cameras open, technical skills beyond me yet—Picasso fixed in stilled motion behind his tenuous centaurs of air. Picasso said of art, "I do not seek. I find."*[2] *I remember the fawn we found, white-spotted and tender-fleshed, flattening itself beneath our gentle touch, grass blade and ivory flower petal smaller than our smallest finger stilled in its eyes, in the deepening of its body where night and owl murmur and elk still secreted themselves in the pliant wrench of bones.*

Late Summer Wasps

(And Not Bees)

Bee foraging bluebeard near my suburban porch.

*When taken out, the plate does not at first appear to have received
a definite impression—some short processes, however,
develop it in the most miraculous beauty.*
—Edgar Allan Poe, "The Daguerreotype," 1840.[1]

My ears are thick with them, the yellow jackets levitating out of this vole hole to hover through our scarecrows of gold banner and harebell. *Murmuration* is a word, even without the starlings' imprint above the leaf light. It is almost too beautiful to write here: the birds I cannot see clustering at night beneath the Milky Way, river of light, their absence silence, the wet leaves, the pulpy flies, the destroying angels I've walked through. I find the wasps perilously close to the cabin path, ferrying small crumbs of red rock into the air, and think them ground diggers. I try to take a picture of them, yellow and black-masked, levitating in and out of the small hole in the ground I marked with a broken pole, the nest beneath it, I learn only later, maybe four feet deep, every minute dozens of frenetic wasps entering, leaving, hovering near-sighted at the hole of it to memorize their place in the world. These yellow jackets fly in and out of the metal sky into the dark cupboards of earth, thousands, while I plunge my arms—this moment, now, again— through bees snout-deep in late blossom, everything and me until the first glittering frost alive.

Raindrop from pine reflecting aspens northside of cabin.

The 19th-century poet and writer, Edgar Allan Poe called the daguerreotype the "most extraordinary triumph of modern science." He believed that under the most powerful microscope a work of ordinary art made by human hands would lose any semblance to nature, while the "photogenic" drawing—photogenic related to "Greek words signifying 'sunpainting'"— reveals "only a more absolute truth, a more perfect identity . . . with the thing represented." And though Poe might argue that all language must fall short of conveying any "just idea of the truth," I find truth here and "miraculous beauty" perhaps in the wasps, written now all noun and verb.

Sweeping Dead Moths from a Window Screen

Western Tanager watching me above the cabin feeder.

I, for whom my grandmother was still myself,
I had never seen her save in my soul . . .
—Marcel Proust, *The Guermantes Way*, 1920.[1]

Lighter than ravens are the moths pelting at the windows where sometimes they spin out when I half-close the window frames. Tonight, the homestead neighbors wash the dark trees we share to nudes, their security lights unblinking beneath Orion's belt in the faded ether. Such a long silence we sometimes share through the winter glaze and I wonder what will bring rescue, pour succor over our bowed heads. The ravens swung past early this morning, hooked themselves to long sheaves of wind that bore them past the hill brow. Roland Barthes, the semiologist who wanted to understand the "newness" of photography and its prick at the soul (my words), asked how meaning gets into image and where does it end? Sometimes, I catch moths in the clear bell of a glass or in my fists where I feel their little heart-thumps before I shake them out into the night air—what moves within me, frayed and jittering down to my broken porch steps. Barthes, when he wrote *Camera Lucida*, grieved for his dead mother and looked into photographs of her "for the truth of the face [he]had loved." Mornings, I sweep shattered things into the world, images or not, "resurrection," as Barthes said, or not, and then rescue the bird feeders that something overnight flings to the ground, repair what I can or not, like a map of the day I keep drawing.

Kestrel watching me from tree near the river outdoor mall.

When a photographer entered the bedroom of Proust's grandmother to take her "death photo," Proust's grandmother, who had always been seen "through [Proust's] transparent sheets of contiguous, overlapping memory," is transformed to Proust's horror into "a dejected old woman whom I did not know." But unlike Proust, I've found those transparent sheets of memory can bring other images of light and the beautiful we barely grasp. There is something oriental for me in both these bird pictures, something beautiful: the accidental placement of the tree branch, the pine twig hanging down to the left of the western tanager, the dot of light in the kestrel's eye I didn't create. I feel seen in these pictures: birds, messengers between worlds, watching me as I watch them.

Western Painted Turtles Sunning

On the Submerged Tree my friend Called Holy

Western Painted Turtles at Eaglewatch Lake by the South Platte River.

Photography is only a new road from a different direction but moving toward the common goal, which is Life.
—Paul Strand, *"Photography," 1917.*

The western tanagers sometimes congregate on the dawn-carved hills south and east of our cabin meadow, a percolation of burnt orange and lemon I wander beneath. I hear them first: a crystalline piping, an allegro of notes in the high octaves of the piano I worried over as a child. I flick at camera dials and buttons in hopes of snagging correct aperture and foci to catch them. I think about faith a lot out there, a kind of sideways meditation. Sometimes when the river in the suburbs is all green leaf light and late summer drought grass, I ask myself, *What have I /what will I /weep over again and again?* I have seen pictures of fathers and their babies draped over their shoulders drowned in river beds across borders. In Ohio, we grew up to tales of hummingbirds that never slept, never touched earth, that bird song is whatever the human mouth can push out with its thick tongue and hard teeth. A landscape photographer once said, "[P]hotography is the story I fail to put into words."[1] Soon the red-winged blackbirds that clang and scrape along the drainage ditches will migrate south of the river here. Everything seeding now, everything floating. When the rain lifts from the clay in the suburbs, I feel it—the bee, thick-thighed and oblivious, whirling its yellow baskets of sweet pollen to places long past only the children know: the tumbled fences of their neighbors left behind or the wheel of a wheelbarrow that someone has pushed against a wall, torn and humming that I keep hearing.

Chickadee feeding on the sunflower in our suburban front garden.

Dorothea Lange was one of the photographers tasked with documenting the plight of the agriculture worker during the Great Depression and Dust Bowl.[2] *She took her now iconic photographs at a pea farm of a migrant mother and her children forced to eat frozen peas out of the fields and small birds killed by the children. I have seen Lange's photograph, "Migrant Mother," many times, the migrant mother and her children protected from the elements by a smattering of canvas as she looks out into space, her hand hooked at her chin, a child on either side, their heads burrowed into her shoulders. Susan Sontag calls photography, "an elegiac art, a twilight art."*[3] *What is beautiful is already filled with pathos because time has passed, decay descended, the door opened. Why don't you take photos of people? Leonard asks me. I have none yet, the images I carry of people in memory only, nothing that I have taken out of time, though what I write, as Susan Sontag says, is simply interpretation, like that image of the father*[4] *and his infant daughter drowned at the river I keep remembering and the bee I heard in the wheel of a wheelbarrow once and then thought of that country of the lost where I have never been.*

Photographing a Cabbage White Butterfly
at Castlewood Canyon

Cabbage White butterfly I photographed in lieu of birds.

We must remember that a photograph can hold just as much as we put into it...
—Ansel Adams, "A Personal Credo," *1943.*[1]

I suppose it was the name, (not the butterfly's), that caught me first: Silk Road. Then the butterfly's, lowly "cabbage-eater" I keep imagining clinging white-winged and green speckle-eyed to a shining hem or a sleeve woven from a silk cocoon some ancient silk farmer boiled just before the silk worm's emergence. That strand of silk, kept intact by that farmer's boiling, could be spun longer than this walking path in a sunken canyon, itself millions of years old. And that Silk Road? Some seven thousand miles away and gone centuries with ancient dynasties and Ottoman Empires and Xanadu courts and an ancient farmer eating a boiled silkworm and a cabbage white butterfly stowing itself away across worlds in tall ships and iron horses to be, here, with me. No wonder Leonard calls me from sleep at three a.m., no moon for a poet, to stand groggy and awed on a cabin porch beneath a universe called *Observable*, despite the billions of galaxies we still can't see spiraling over the Milky Way—*Scattered Straw, Silver River, Way of Birds*. It's the cabbage white butterfly I am thinking of because a Master Birder told me of beautiful birds in a canyon and I went to catch the singing White-throated Swift or the Lazuli Bunting or the Plumbeous Vireo I could hang in a simple black frame by my kitchen window. But all I could find was a butterfly, plain as a moth and hanging upside down on a purple weed I couldn't name. Instar is a molting, I have read, for something new every time the cabbage white butterfly's exoskeleton sheds. Now the head black. Now the yellow clypeus of the face. Now those green eye dots I love.

Grass Skipper foraging at Castlewood Canyon.

I should have shooed this grass skipper from the tiny flower it grasped just to see it move through the canyon, skipping from blade to blade between the rocks. Instead, I took a picture, blind before now to its dark pebble eye and the orange club on the end of its antenna. The photographer Man Ray created his images on photographic paper without a camera: the shadow of the object creating the image—light and shadow more important than the picture. He called his images "oxidized residues, fixed by light."[2] This is the picture I posted on Facebook where someone said, and I don't know why, "I see a book." Man Ray believed that desire awakens with "the first gesture of a child," who seeing an object only names it, but beneath that naming is "a world of intended meaning."

And so I wrote.

Catching Light

Young bull elk gazing north in the dying aspen grove past Jan's picnic table.

*What amazingly fine education this continued search for the very quintessence of life
—the poetry of being—to have to seize unhesitatingly and make final at once in the silver emulsion...*
—Edward Weston, "Random Notes on Photography," 1922.

"What We've Lost: The Species Declared Extinct," *2020*.
—*Scientific American*

I walked out this morning into the sodden grass, still name-less to me sometimes, heavy from the night's rain, the golden light I'd come with my camera to shoot fractured and paling. Last night, I read that there are some species so lost in time that there is no common name to list for them, like the beautifully named, like *Dusty Sea Snake* or *Long-Spine Bream* or *Lily-of-the-Valley-Tree*. All summer, before my half-stepping here through these fields, the grasshopper sparrows darted white-tailed in front of me, floating just beyond the dark canopies of grass I have learned to drape back so carefully, fearful of the newly-born, their freckled eggs broken, the frog-mouthed nestlings gone now but for these words. *Golden Mole* or *Sheetweb Weaver*, *Tall Thimbleweed*: what have I mourned that's lost? A mother's life? A child's love? The roar and whistle of a bull elk zippers over the trees through golden light. Somewhere, my hunting neighbors haunt their little acres of woods as if the gods had turned them from men to trees, to camouflage and coyote urine, to blue metal rifles and muzzle-loaders. The bull elk calls and so I blow, as a child does, as I did once, past a blade of grass held tight between my thumbs, something like the sound of broken glass silencing the jays then, something like yearning. I hold my eye against the camera's eye and wait, crouched here for I don't know how long beneath the long-limbed aprons of the trees. Soon, the bull elk will wander in from the east, what I want to save, and it will gaze to the north, all lazy torpor amid the sun spill, its rack of years I will count and count lit up. So beautiful and named this elk I keep finding in the heartbreak of these firing leaves, in this list of the lost I keep carrying. Cold and metal-smooth the air the elk and I will breathe until I open the camera's shutter to fix the shadows, *the most transitory of things*, William Henry Fox Talbot once said, with light.[1]

It seems right that my journey into photography would come back to William Henry Fox Talbot, father of photogenic drawings or calotypes: names rooted in the Greek words for "beautiful" and "type." All through this I kept finding my way back to Talbot, his joy and amazement at the "fairy pictures, creations of a moment" that his camera cast on paper and then faded. His invention, what he thought captured the "pencil of nature" through a beam of light was usurped by the silver-washed copper plates of Louis Daguerre: exposure and a "perfect image of nature" quickened in a mere three to thirty minutes. What image to leave here? Perfected by mechanics, imbued by the human soul? In 1931, Walter Benjamin looked back through the history of photography, a discovery that set fire to a world of art that believed in the hand of God through the hand of the artist inspired and not the shutter or glass lens. In his concluding remarks, his writerly life coming forth, Benjamin asked if captions would not become "the essential component of pictures?" Through the caption would photos, once seemingly isolated and disconnected from the human and the godly, become literature and the photograph no longer "bound in coincidences?" Perhaps that is what I have pursued here: my photos filled with, as Talbot says, "the numerous details" I did not have time, at the moment of seeing, to write down, now the photographic image ferrying me to image and memory, an art "in which light creates its own metaphors."² An art in which whole worlds are fixed in light. Beautiful. That word again.

Dream bird from the San Diego Zoo I cannot name.

Study Guide

1. Look at the cover photograph for *This Visible Speaking* entitled, "Two Ducks Swimming Eaglewatch Lake beneath a Tree Called Holy." Why do you think I felt like this photograph was the photograph to represent the whole book and Dante's concept of "visible speaking" (see the preface for Dante's quote and what he says about "visible speaking")? How might the photograph metaphorically represent this idea of visible speaking?

2. The art of Ekphrastic writing (vivid description of a visual object) is said to have been part of the writing world since Homer first described so richly the forging of the shield of Achilles in the *Iliad* about three thousand years ago. A simple definition of the ekphrastic is a detailed description of a visual work of art, written through prose or poetry. Do the prose pieces in *This Visible Speaking* work as ekphrastic pieces? Why and Why not? You can check out *The Ekphrastic Review* for more information on ekphrastic writing https://www.ekphrastic.net/

3. The images in this book are not only the visual images in the photographs but also the written images. There is an old adage in poetry, "Show, Don't Tell." Choose a few written images in the book and brainstorm on what you think the images are showing, and telling.

4. An important part of the book are the voices of past photographers and those who write about the beginning of photography. We hear their questions, excitement, and wariness about the dawn of photography and the new age of visual art it promised. What do these voices bring to the rest of the book? How do they interact with the photographs and the prose poems?

5. An epigraph is a short line or sentence at the beginning of a book or a poem or a prose piece. *This Visible Speaking* begins with an epigraph by Jacob Burckhardt, considered the founding father of art history. Each section has its own epigraph before the prose poem. How do those epigraphs set up for the reader a possible way to read the book and each section? Choose an epigraph and discuss how you see it working in conversation with the prose poem and the whole chapter.

Acknowledgments

Thanks first to poet Robert Cooperman, a Facebook friend, who first mentioned the word, "book." Thanks to those friends over the past few years who have cheered me on in my photography and my writing: Juliet Beckman, Lucy Graca, Annie Dawid, Carol Guerrero-Murphy, and, of course, Leonard. Thanks to my good friends Steve Harvey and Robert Root at *The Humble Essayist Press* who cheered me on and said, "Yes!" when I tentatively put forth the idea of *This Visible Speaking*. Thanks, Robert, for the wonderful edits and suggestions and for your wonderful foreword to the book, "This Visible Speaking: An Introduction." I always learn from you. Thank you to *The Tiny Seed Journal* for choosing the text for "Photographing The Wild Geranium," published in its *Poetry of the Wild Flowers Anthology*. Thank you to Jasmine Chu for choosing my photograph, "Morning Surprise!," of a mother great horned owl with her owlet on the back cover of this book for "The Passionate Spectator: Photography Exhibit at Children's Hospital." Thanks to my old colleague, John Hall, for his graphic design help with the book cover. Thanks to publisher and poet friend Jonah Bornstein for his timely advice during the production of this book. Thanks to Will Sardinsky for the fun photo of me and Millie. And thank you, finally, to Kitty and John for that surprise Christmas gift and the beautiful world you opened!

About the Author

Millie and Me
Photo by Will Sardinsky

Kathryn Winograd has been a poet since she stood in front of her mother seated at the typewriter and recited her poems for a contest, while her mother frantically typed. (She believes she won third place for her poem about a lonely swan floating in the velvet sky.) Since then, Winograd has received a Master of Fine Arts degree from the Iowa Writer's Workshop and a Ph.D. from the University of Denver. Her poetry has won awards and Pushcart nominations, including the Colorado Book Award in Poetry, and has been published in places as disparate as *The New Yorker* and *Cricket Magazine for Kids*. While teaching in the low residency Poetry and Creative Nonfiction MFA program for Ashland University, the universe gave the poet Winograd a dope slap and she began writing creative nonfiction. Her most recent collection of creative nonfiction essays, *Slow Arrow: Unearthing the Frail Children*, was awarded a Bronze Meadow in Essay for the Independent Publisher Book Awards. Like her poems, Winograd's essays have been published in numerous places such as *River Teeth, Fourth Genre, Hotel Amerika,* and *Terrain.org*. A Christmas gift of a camera by her daughter and son-in-law opened up a new adventure and Winograd has since published cover photographs for literary journals and online essays and poems. Recently, her first photograph was accepted into a gallery exhibit and sold.

Endnotes

Preface

1. Julia Margaret Cameron digitized, unfinished biography, *Annals of My Glass House*, can found online at the Victoria and Albert Museum website: https://www.vam.ac.uk/

2. Ekphrasis, a vivid description of a work of art, dates back to Horace, a Roman lyric poet from the time of Augustus. (65BC-8BC)

3. Newhall, Beaumont, editor. *Photography: Essays & Images: Illustrated Readings in the History of Photography*. Museum of Modern Art, 1980.

4. Trachtenberg, Alan, editor. *Classic Essays on Photography*. Leete's Island Books, 2005.

5. From William Henry Fox Talbot's, "Some Account of the Art of Photogenic Drawing," *1839*. Talbot, scientist and linguist in the 1800s, was one of the first men to experiment with fixing light image on paper, using a camera lucida. A slower technique than M. Louis Daguerre's, his process never became popular.

6. Oliver Wendell Holmes was a 19th-century physician and enthusiastic amateur photographer who published articles on the photogenic technique.

7. Charles Baudelaire, a French poet,(*Les Fleurs du mal : The Flowers of Evil*) decried the rise of photography and the artists' emulation of it, fearing pragmatism in art rather than dream and emotion.

8. 19th-century poet Edgar Allen Poe was one of the first to write about the daguerreotype: "perhaps the most extraordinary triumph of modern science."

Unlocking the Camera

1. From "The First News Accounts of the Daguerreotype," *La Gazette de France, January 6, 1839*.

2. From Edward Weston's "Random Notes on Photography," 1922. Edward Weston is one of America's most famous 20th-century photographers, known for his work in black and white and his focus on the American West.

3. From Roland Barthes' *Camera Lucida*, Chapter 37. Roland Barthes, French essayist and literary theorist, wrote *Camera Lucida* in an attempt to understand the significance of one photo of his mother.

4. From William Henry Fox Talbot's, *The Open Door*, The MET Photographs Collection.

On Beauty and Finding a Dead Flicker

1. Albert Sands Southworth opened Southworth and Hawes studio in 1843 and created hundreds of aesthetically beautiful daguerreotypes.

2. From Charles Baudelaire's, "On Photography," from The Salon of 1859.

Owl Head at Beaver Creek

1. Dominique François Arago, the French Minister of the Interior, proposed to the French Government to buy the rights to the daguerreotype from M. Daguerre, solving the problem of obtaining a patent for an invention made out of common everyday materials.

2. Paul *Valéry*, a French Symbolist poet, believed photographs could give writers the physical reality that they might have missed with their own eyes.

Photographing the Wild Geranium

1. Alfred Stieglitz, a modern American photographer and husband to the paiter Georgia O'Keeffe, emphasized the craftmanship in photography as a way to legitimize it as an art.

2. From Paul Rosenfeld's review of Alfred Stieglitz's 1921 photograph exhibit, an exaltation of his work, simply entitled, "Stieglitz." Available through Hathitrust.

3. Georgia O'Keeffe is a beloved American painter known for beautiful and what some think of as sometimes sexualized portraits of flowers, vegetables, bones, and sea shells, among other things.

4. From Stieglitz's letters written to O'Keeffe, collected by Sarah Greenough in *My Faraway One* and excerpted by NPR.

Moth Orchid at the Botanical Gardens

1. Henry Peach Robinson became known for his portraitures, using multiple negatives to create one image.

2. From *National Geographic*: Naledi, little star, is the name given to the child whose teeth were found on a ledge deep in the Rising Star cave.

3. From Man Ray's, "The Age of Light," 1934. Man Ray was an American painter, as well as a photographer, who created his own camera-less pictures through light and treated paper, calling them *rayographs*.

4. From Walter Benjamin's, "A Short History of Photography," 1931. Benjamin, a German philosopher and literary critic, believed that art criticism must center on the work, not the artist's life. A Jewish exile to Paris during the start of Hitler's reign, Benjamin killed himself at the French/Spanish border to escape return to Paris and certain death.

Our Rock Blossom Blooms

1. Frederick H. Evans, a British photographer known for his images of medieval cathedrals, believed in the strict accuracy of a photo with no manipulations, unlike the pictorialists, who stressed beauty over accuracy.

2. From "Photography and the New God" (1922). Paul Strand, a modern American photographer, who, after Alfred Stieglitz criticized his unfocused photographs, experimented with street movement to create the first abstractions using a camera.

3. From Edward Weston's, "Seeing Photographically", 1965.

4. From "Spring and All."

3 a.m. and Taking the Puppy for a Pee Beneath a New Moon

1. American photographer Berenice Abbott objected to the manipulations of the photograph to make it more like the painting, citing Photo-Secession as a radical turning from what should be pure photography. Photography as a documentary should be true, informative, and part of the "pulse of the day."

2. From The Fine Arts *A New Discovery* printed in the La Gazette de France on January 6, 1839.

3. From *Biography.com*.

Finding a Paper Wasp Nest Hanging Below a Porch Beam

1. John Berger was a 20th-century British art critic and novelist famous for his BBC series, *Ways of Seeing*, and his book, *Understanding a Photo*. According to Berger, photography "has no language of its own," simply preserving a moment from time, and making what is not shown as important as what is.

Scrawled Cowfish Found on a Childhood Beach

1. Lady Elizabeth Eastlake was a mid-century writer on art who saw photography as merely mechanical and its images not indicative of man's creative power.

2. From William M. Ivins, Jr.'s, "New Reports and New Visions: The Nineteenth Century," 1953. William M. Ivins, Jr. was the first curator of the Prints department for the Metropolitan Museum in New York.

Two Owls Dip Down from a Ponderosa Pine

1. From Walter Benjamin's, "A Short History of Photography," 1931. David Octavius Hill was a 19th-century Scottish Painter and Photographer.

2. From an unsigned piece published 1908 in *Camera Work: A Photographic Quarterly*, an art journal created and published by Alfred Stieglitz.

Histogram of the Fox in My Backyard

1. St Francis of Assisi is the patron saint of animals and the environment.

2. Bazin believed that painting had two ambitions, "expression of spiritual reality" and "duplication of the world outside."

Drawing with Light

1. Pablo Picasso was one of the most influential artists in modern times.

2. From *Oxford Reference: in Signature III* (1936) Graham Sutherland "A Trend in English Draughtsmanship"

Late Summer Wasps

1. Edgar Allan Poe marveled at the daguerreotype's technology and process for producing a picture, as well as its promise of surpassing "the wildest expectations of the most imaginative."

Sweeping Dead Moths from a Window Screen

1. From *Proust Ink.com*. Marcel Proust, one of the most important writers of the 20th-century French novel, explored the power of art to withstand the destructive forces of time

Western Painted Turtles Sunning

1. From https://www.destinsparks.com/links/photography-quotes/. Destin Sparks, landscape photographer based out of Australia

2. From Dorothea Lange's, "The Assignment I'll Never Forget," 1960. Lange, famous for her photograph, "Migrant Mother," almost passed by the Pea Picker Camp where the mother and her children lived in a crude lean-to. The photographer, Lange said, must have passion and "inner compulsion" in her work in order to reach the greatest depths in her photography.

3. Writer and Critic Susan Sontag wrote the book, *On Photography* (2001), which won the National Book Critics' Circle Award for Criticism for its exploration into the role of photography in society.

4. Óscar Alberto Martínez Ramírez and his 23-month-old daughter, Valeria, were attempting to cross the river into United States. The photo of their bodies drowned in the river made headlines across the world on the plight of the desperate migrant.

Photographing a Cabbage White Butterfly

1. Ansel Adams is one of America's best-known photographers and environmentalists known for his photographs of America's natural monuments.

2. From Man Ray's, "The Age of Light," 1934.

Catching Light

1. From William Henry Fox Talbot's, "On the Art of Fixing A Shadow," 1839.

2. From Hubert Damisch's, "Five Notes for a Phenomenology Of the Photographic Image," 1963. A modern art historian and French philosopher, Damisch disagreed with the prevailing theory that artwork conveyed the artist's intentions. He believed that each art piece has its own "pictorial intelligence."

Printed in the USA
CPSIA information can be obtained
at www.ICGtesting.com
LVRC091143200324
774976LV00008B/69